Timed Out

Essence of Time Management

Attention Authors

Manas Publications is fighting a war to tell the world that India can win the battle not only by the bullet but also by the pen. We are converting fighters into writers. There is no dearth of intellectuals in our country, however, their knowledge is confined to them only. No sincere effort has been made by any other publisher to give the right direction to their knowledge and the talent of every intellectual is lying hidden. An author always presents the raw material in the shape of a manuscript and it is the job of the publisher to convert it to a finished product. Manas has been continually motivating intellectuals and publishing their manuscripts for more than two decades and would like to publish your manuscript too. If you or your colleagues have a manuscript ready for publication or are working on it, contact us with a detailed synopsis and list of contents. Manas will also suggest you a suitable title for writing related to your area of expertise. Manas is known for its publishing quality. We take utmost care in publishing and also give wide publicity to the book and its author through our national and international distribution network.

Timed Out

Essence of Time Management

Col. M.S. Jaswal

Manas Publications
New Delhi-110002 (INDIA)

MANAS PUBLICATIONS
(We Convert Fighters into Writers)
(Publishers, Library Suppliers, Importers & Exporters)
4402/5-A, Ansari Road (Opp. HDFC Bank)
Darya Ganj, New Delhi-110 002 (India)
Off. (23260783, 23265523, Fax: 011-23272766
E-mail: manaspublications@vsnl.com
manaspublications@gmail.com

New Impression 2015

ISBN 978-81-7049-338-9

₹ 295/-

Designed at

Manas Publications

Printed in India at
HS Offsets, Delhi
and published by Mrs Suman Lata for
Manas Publications, 4402/5-A,
Ansari Road, (Opp. HDFC Bank),
Darya Ganj, New Delhi-110 002 (INDIA)

Preface (Time Truths)

I offer no magical mantras of salvation, for I have none.

I quote none of the known management gurus for I have read none of them.

I am not appended to any sage to offer his words of wisdom.

I myself am not a very learned man.

I do offer quotes of learned men and from a few sacred books.

I only offer my humble thoughts. They come straight from my heart.

I offer solution to overcome the trivialities of your mismanaged life.

I firmly believe that the mismanaged life stems out from mismanaging your precious time. I, just over a period of time, have firmed in my acute explanation on this most crucial aspect of time, which shapes our lives. ***Time is the destiny shaper of your life***. These are trivial observations, spread over the span of my life, some passed down in the classical Indian style from a father to a son, and some based on my discriminating observations.

We have only one life to live. In this timeframe, we have to achieve whatever we have set ourselves to accomplish. This book tries to tabulate those observations in a simple analytical form. It is my endeavour to help make life more stimulating and purposeful.

We have often heard the famous quip: My life is bushed. I did not make it in race of life. I am out of time, where is the time, I have no time. And time! Wish I had it.

It happens daily in our lives and it will happen in nine counts out of ten.

It will happen, for we all are human.

It will happen repeatedly, for we do not plan our life.

It will happen, for we are not trained to time our life.

On nine counts out of ten, in the act of living life, we will always be timed out.

Universe moves in motion of time. ***We are time trapped***. The big bang four billion years ago created what we savour today. A bigger bang four billion years from now may take away all those things we savour today. This acute phenomenon was well understood by our seers and sages ages back. ***Time is not elastic. It cannot be stretched. Time is a constant***. It is a constant unpleasant fact of life. In addition, more importantly the constant time one perceives is a ***constant diminishing dimension***. It has a beginning and a foreseeable end. ***The day you were born, you were destined to die***. That is your life span of time. When both ends of the spectrum are visible then to manage the space in between is in your own hands and our own homework and a definite task. The more you waste time, the more quickly it diminishes in reality.

Guess what happens when you do not complete any task given in the school, work place or even at home. One gets a rough stick. It is similar with time. ***You fool around with time; it will fool around with you.***

Have we ever analysed what happens when we fool around with time. To know about this aspect a little more, take your mind to the wandering sages, steeped in wisdom of life. They glow, their faces glow, they live legendary hundred years, they practise the art repeatedly, and they practise the ***art of taming the time***. Yoga, the ultimate bliss in physical and spiritual exercise, aims and has one central physical exercise theme, breathe easy, and breathe in time and not out of it. When you focus your breathing to perform in conjunction with induced muscular spasms, we get the maximum benefit in Yoga.

All the ills that manifest in our body are due to improper management of time. Heart attacks, nervous breakdowns, rashes, breathlessness, diabetes, stones and what not; what one can pick up from medical mumbo-jumbo are the products of sheer mismanagement of your precious time. You eat trash to save time, you eat while running to office, you eat in your car, and you eat while going to office, the result, obesity or diabetes and repeat it over a long period of time, the result, a heart attack.

Why do we humans not plan time or in fact plan our life. Can we live without it? I think and most of us feel that we can. We think time has no end. We do not have that ability to see the distant horizon. We all have studied the success stories of great people. Take any one from the pages of history, say Alexander the Great or Isaac Newton. Each individual valued the ***value of time***. They knew what it was, how precious it was and how best it would be to exploit it. It was ***treated as a science*** and science seldom lies.

We all, in our hectic life are whipped by the pain of daily living. We cut corners, make do things and regret or rue our decisions later. To undo a wrong we spend more time, which we could have used better at the very first instance, had we planned our time.

Time management has to be treated as a ***philosophy of life***. Some even call it ***life management***. Yes, we do need to manage time to effectively manage our lives. It is essential that all aspect of our lives, whether they be spiritual, physical, mental, emotional, social, material, love, child rearing, home keeping, personal investments or professional time requirements, they all need to be managed and balanced in a way that you achieve the most satisfying results. ***Time is the core of happiness***. You mess up one, the other will pile up on you and the burden of bad time management will weigh you down. Do you want to be rebuked by your children that you were never there when they wanted you the most. You want the divorcing wife to say that you never pay attention to her. Your friends do not call up when you are down, for when they were down you never had time to be with them. Your boss calls you an idiotic nincompoop, for your work is never complete.

Here in Defence Services, from where I hail professionally from, the essence of time, clockwork precision, tight timetables and stringent schedules are the bed rock on which any worthwhile army is bred upon. ***Time management is the cannon fodder of professionalism***. As a layman observer how do you assess any organisation is working in the pink of health. Check their offices. Do they open in time or do the staff members come in time? Then check its end product, that do their services are attended in time their products are delivered in time? If all issues are better in time management than the competing company, then blindly invest in the better time managed company. ***Time is the key.*** Can a soldier attack before the pre-designated hour? Can the artillery lift its bombardment before time? If they both indulge in time mismanagement then valuable human lives will be lost. ***Time is the support system of life.*** One cannot do a thing earlier or later, for ***you are fixed in the spectrum of time***. Can your two-year old child drive a car? I do not think he can.

I feel myself blessed to have had the privilege of being with three seers for a very brief period in my life. Let me narrate my experiences with them.

The first was a renowned yogi. Before joining National Defence Academy, I discovered that I had a squint in my eyes and they were two points weak. One recommended exercise by the yogi, my six months of dedicated effort to do it and till today I am 6 by 6 in my eyesight with no squint. On knowing that I was joining the Army, he that day lovingly demonstrated what he called American PT. With one push from his hands, he would rise minimum one foot from ground along with his feet, parallel to the ground. ***Timing the thoughts and muscles to perform in synergy was the key***, he said.

Despite murderous PT in my whole life, I have not been able to replicate that feat. What I learnt through that experience was that **if you are dedicated to a cause and synchronise your mind with muscles to make them dance in tango with time, you can achieve your objective.**

Second was an IAS man who had renounced the world in service of Shri Sainath. My mother took me to him to drill some spiritual sense into her otherwise not so God-fearing son. I sat in one corner of the room murmuring, in my mind, the only shloka of incantation to Lord Shiva I knew. The learned man came to me, peeped into my eyes, smiled and said, "When you have Shiva in your heart you need leanings on no other." I was stunned. My second learning was **if you condition your mind and brain to one focus of thoughts, they get imprinted over your body cover and come true.**

The third was with Baba Ji of Beas, whom I bumped in-to accidentally in my sisters' house. I caught him explaining to someone the difficulty in attaining spirituality. He gave a very simple example. To a man enclosed in one room for his entire life, the only source of light would be the bulb, which shines. If that man was asked what was the source of light he would point to the shining bulb. Within his own perception of things, that entrapped man is right and cannot be wrong. Only when he steps out of the enclosed room will he realise how wrong he was. The source of light to the earth is sun. Only when he transcends the spatial boundaries of the Solar system will he realise how diminutive his thoughts were, when he was in referring to the sun, as the only source of light. I learnt another lesson that day. **Unless you widen your horizon, you remain fixed to your minuscule self.**

Athletes who finish races behind others do not stand on podium. A few who do stand on the podium, are those very few who have utilised their time effectively. ***If we do not use the time effectively, we will be timed out in life.***

Do we need to utilise the time effectively or mull over it that it is a waste of time.

Do we open our mind to new concepts if the old do not seem to be working?

I leave that to the inner beatings of your heart to find the right answer.

☆ ☆ ☆

Contents

☆ ☆ ☆

"Thou art energy, give me energy.
Thou art manliness, Give me manliness.
Thou art strength, give me strength.
Thou art vigour, give me vigour.
Thou art wrath, give me wrath.
Thou art conquering power, give me
conquering power."

— Yajur Veda,
(Verse 19.9)

CHAPTER 1

Pillars of Time Management

I have very deliberately left the most important chapter of this book the shortest.

If these mundane issues do not make any headway in your brain then other parts certainly won't. The few words, which I throw at you, are the essence of reshaping your life with the principles of time management. They are tabulated below.

Time is a Diminishing Constant, Thus is a Very Diminutive Commodity. The rate or the speed of its diminishing dimension is to the power cube to your wasted time on earth in relation to number of desires left unfulfilled. In very simple words, as your end nears, you wished that that confounding time were there to achieve those few goals you could not.

You Have One Life To Live, Thus One Time Span To Achieve. If someone has two lives to live then leave or if you are banking upon science to break the frontier of mortality then still leave. We will be governed by one life for many years to come.

Do You Have The Will To Do It? It is all about training. It takes extra effort and time initially. It is all about that elusive will power to do that something extra. The weak hearted need not break this barrier.

If the above three-line jargon does not make any sense to you then I request the esteemed reader to close the book and not waste his time any further. You may have time to do just that something useful, which you have been dreaming about than to read this book.

☆ ☆ ☆

"Nobody on earth can sit idle,
Without doing a deed,
Or without having any desire."

— Yajur Veda,
(Mantra 48, Chapter 7)

CHAPTER 2

One Life

I am steeped in this five thousand years old culture. In fact, I am ensnared in it.

Being a staunch Hindu, it gives me the unique privilege to interpret my religious texts the way I perceive them. It is the combination of that strength and right, imparted by my five thousand-year old culture to me.

Despite my sacred Gita, which gives me immortality and many lives to live. Despite you, my sacred text, maybe I have not been granted the right ability to see you in proper context. Maybe, I am denied Gyan (Self Knowledge) and live in Agyan (Without Self Knowledge). Maybe, the true light of Yog (Vigyan) to destroy enemies within, has not touched my bodily shores. Maybe, to be free from desire and ego to attain the Supreme Bhava (Feeling for God), so to be completely free from sorrow, birth, death and attain immortality has not dawned on me. Maybe, I will never become the imperishable one. Maybe, my soul will not leave this human body and enter another blessed body. Maybe, in this one life my inner eye you seek to open will remain ever closed. For all the above frailties I seek your forgiveness dear God.

Maybe, I do not want to be tempered by the sayings and interpretations of so many.

Unless we are the manifestations of some gods residing in any nook of this universe, we will live only once.

I do believe mortality is my birthright.

Immortality is an elusive chimera the humans have been chasing endlessly since time. All the living species are governed by this principle of one life. The law of universe is universal in this astuteness. Even the earth was born once, so were the stars and they will die as we can witness the creation we thought endless also sucked into massive black holes of future.

What is your black hole in life?

Do you see one black hole or are oblivious of its existence. I believe that *yama* does come riding his favourite black bull. You may have chosen a different vessel to reach your hell or heaven, but the Satan is not known to miss his time.

Therefore, we know that ***we have just one life to live***. It is the only life you have to achieve something in life. Do you want to die unsung, unknown like million others? You want your successor ten generations later to tell with pride, oh, I hail from that lineage, oh that guy was my great grandpa.

The choice to do so is entirely in our hands. Humans have the most complex brains and it makes choices for existence every second. Even the most mundane creatures make choices. Then why do we humans not make choices, which are in line with basic theories of life. Can we live by breathing nitrogen, maybe yes, in some other planet but definitely not here on earth? Can we live without the sun? Can we live without managing our little available time?

Moreover, what choice do you take to live your life? Read below and take your pick.

One life of being a failure.

One life of shame.

One life of deprivation.

One life of lamenting.

One life of ruing.

One life of unfulfilled wants.

One life of missed chances.

Or

One life of happiness.

One life of fulfilled desires.

One life of accomplishments.

One life of joy.

One life of each second well lived.

One life of head held high and full of senseless pride.

Your one life may have been an accident of pleasure, planned, unplanned or a God sought intervention. You are here baby. You are here to stay baby. You can work or sit idle; you can achieve or be a failure baby. You have arrived in this world baby. I am sure your manliness and pride would not let you engage the friendship of idioms like failure or idle. If that is the case, then you better have a better plan for your life.

Planning for the life is not as difficult as it seems. We plan for everything in life. We plan daily. Even as a child, you planned your piddle and potty breaks. As a young student, you plan your school activities. As a young teen, you plan your clothes, how you look and what you want to eat. As we grow in life, we plan our family. **So planning is an essential requirement with which we exist.**

Proper planning shapes our destiny.

How do we plan? It is simple.

We lay down an aim. Once the aim is clear, you plan to attain it. Now herein lies the problem. You aim at what level, at what height of success.

Here are some valuable hints for planning your aims in life.

Plan in small steps with each horizon visible.

Plan what you can achieve in that time span. Planning for becoming the richest man in the world or to be the top man of your organisation may not be wrong but impractical when you have started your business or joined an organisation a year back. Make a progressive plan, which ascends gradually in the scope of accomplishing your achievements.

Reassess your plans constantly or midway to reassess your targets or set higher ones.

Have two plans in place. One what you want to ultimately achieve in life and what one you at present moment are planning to achieve.

Do not loose hope if you fail to achieve your targets. Reset the aim and recalibrate the targets.

Work hard to achieve your fixed aim. Dreaming an aim and then not working for it will not take you anywhere. Sweat it out for it. It should become a second obsession.

I am an avid military man. That was the life I had chosen and that was what I was interested only in. I did not pass at the top merit of my course. I was a mediocre cadet who just let the life move by, as it wanted to move. On joining my Infantry unit I saw a very marked difference how the organisation and your own soldiers treated a professionally qualified officer. At a very young military age, I promised to myself that I would do well in my mandatory courses of instructions. When others were enjoying an afternoon siesta, I would work on my weapon aspects. Troops loved me, for I showed that extra will to beat the famous Indian May heat with them. I had set a target and was astonished myself when I achieved outstanding grading in all the courses. That fixation of the aim paid. That hard work to remain fixed on that aim paid. I was the first officer to do so in my unit to achieve it.

Fix your aims for your achievements, earlier the better.

Somewhere in my mid life, I desperately wanted to top the most precious Defence Staff Course. Leave alone topping it, I failed to clear it twice. I was shattered. One elusive paper, the very one I used to give people treatise on, I failed with regular monotony. I deemed it to be the end of my military career. I felt doomed. I was a failure in my own eyes. I reassessed the situation and restarted again. Yes. I may not become a general in the Army, but I am where, where most of my doing well course mates have not yet reached.

All is possible, provided you have faith in your abilities.

When I confided to my wife, almost four years back, that I wanted to pen a military fiction, novel, she almost fell off the chair laughing. It egged me on to do it. It took me four years to write and publish my first novel, *Crimson Kashmir*. It took me another two years to pen my second military fiction novel, *Kargil Knot*. It will definitely take me less than a year to pen this third book, *Timed Out*. I have a long-term aim for my writing career, which I discovered due to a taunt of the woman I dearly love. I plan to write ten books in my life span. The idea is not to make any positive dent in my financial standing. It was to just write and publish my first novel. It was to just see that pride in my son's eyes once again, when he quipped; oh, my father wrote a novel. Moreover, this time he gave me a very serious suggestion, dad please do some publicity. It is to see that happiness in my mother's eyes when her eyes rest on my first novel in the library at our farmhouse.

Do not make the mistake to equate your dreams to the finances gained. Then you will never be able to live your dream. Be ready to spend to achieve them if you have to. For financial health, you have your career to live for.

Your dreams or desires generally eat your finances.

My aims are short and long. One book at a time, to write ten books in total. Numerous friends of mine were curious to know how much time I spent. When I told four years for the first novel, almost all said not worth the effort for they conceived that you did nothing else, but wrote, day in and day out for four years. How wrong one can be in one's perception. I have very big aim sliced into small aims, which are achievable, if you just pen one page a day.

Chop the bigger picture into digestible slices.

Happiness in me was immense when a young officer working with me and motivated himself to write his first management book, *You Can't Punch With a Thumb.* It took him a day to reset his beliefs and convert the newfound conviction into action.

When you are focused and positive about life, you rub the goodness onto others.

To achieve what you have set yourself to do, you need a set of desires. ***These desires will act as stepping-stones to ultimately accomplish your aim.*** Now desires are very strange in constitution. There are positive desires, which impart goodness as you trudge forward in life. They have positive influence on your body and mind and those next to you. There are also negative desires, which do not allow you to cull your expertise. They could be anger, jealousy, obsession, materialism etc. Generally, one finds more negative desires manifesting themselves in your body than the positive ones. As for myself, I till date have not been able to negate my negative desires of gluttony and having fatherly patience with my hyperactive kids. Maybe, I have not tried hard enough. One has to reach a fine balance between these desires to let you move forward and not pull you back in life.

Mahatma Gandhi was once asked, "When will you be happy." He replied, "When I am rid of all my desires." He was following the Buddha's philosophy in life of curtailing your desires to attain enlightenment. The central thought remains the same in both the great learned men of their times, both separated by thousands of years of cultural and scientific gap. Reduce your desires or fulfil them earliest that you have no desires. Only then, will you get happiness or attain enlightenment.

I am magically pulled back and can never forget a line from my favourite poem *'If'* authored by Rudyard Kipling. I am not ashamed to admit, that, I have that, 'if' genetic defect. The poem used to hang by in our rooms in the National Defence Academy. In my times of doom and gloom (which were many during the training period of three years), one scan of those lines of wisdom, would uplift your downtrodden thoughts and mind. My favourite stanza written by the author to his son were,

> **"If you can fill the unforgiving minute,**
> **With sixty seconds worth of distance run.**
> **Yours is the Earth and everything that's in it,**
> **And, which is more. you will be a Man, my son."**

Have we run or have you run your time with all that worth?

Most of us just jog.

Most of us just walk.

Most of us just sit.

Most of us just sleep.

It is time we started running the distance with times worth.

For, if we do not, then we are most likely to waste our lives, fall into time trap and will be timed out.

My first simple solution, for you is to set an aim to achieve in life.

☆ ☆ ☆

THINGS YOU NEED TO DO

- Formulate Your Aim In Life.
- Tabulate Your Positive Desires which Take You Forward.
- Tabulate Your Negative Desires, Which Pull You Backwards.

"Regret for wasted time is more wasted time."

— Mason Cooley

CHAPTER 3

Hi, High Life

I am trapped in this world. However I wish, I cannot live away from this earth and its earthlings.

My discourse thus, is centred around what we frail humans, in body and mind, perceive in reality of this life. I will not endeavour to take you on a spiritual plane, which defies the basics of reality. Nor is the aim to make you spiritual appended to any religion of thought. I will let you discover your own God. For you are the Brahma (The God) and you decide what is right for you to do.

Hi, is an universal abridged slang word world over, for a more formal word 'hello'. Hello is uttered, to connect two unknown ends, to connect to strangers, on meeting friends. The word has a worldwide appeal for it emits warmth, it displays heartfelt happiness, it reflects goodness and it shows the sincerity of fair and honest intentions. It postulates the desire to embrace.

Yes, hi is to embrace.

We embrace almost always good things in life.

What happens when one embraces good things in life? When you do so, you do not think twice, it comes on naturally, you do not consult your friends or parents, it brings instantaneous happiness, your face bursts in joy, there is that bounce in your steps, it becomes the simple magic love potion of your existence, it adds value to your existence, it increases your life , you feel uniquely satisfied and you feel high.

Do you always embrace good things in your life?

Let us for a moment dwell on its stark naked and opposite side. What happens when you embrace bad things in life? Do you naturally tell your children to do something similar? Bad things make you wince, you do it on sly, you hide that aspect from the prying eyes of your friends and near ones, you don't go about on a chest beating spree, you keep quite about it, you exclude your friends from it, your eyes do not rise, you generally become a singular introvert and most importantly you loose out in life.

The eulogy to goodness, which I tabled before you, was only to bring forward an important point. You must say hi to or embrace good things in life, naturally and be proud of them.

Say hi, hi to high life.

High life?

I am certainly not referring to the elevated terrain you have chosen to live at, to be nearer to the gods in heaven above.

I am talking about high life.

What is high life?

High life is a state of life you choose to live in. It is the inner state of your happiness with life. It is your satisfaction with life. It is your love for life. It is the mental equilibrium of your sanity. It is your internal ode to life; a prayer of having been blessed with this one life.

When do you feel high in life?

You feel high in life when good things happen to you. You feel high in life when happiness surrounds you. You feel high in life when success hounds your each step. You feel high in life when all your spiritual, materialistic, social and physical parameters are met as per the exacting standards set by you. You feel high in life when you feel you have lived your life well. You feel high when you are nearer to your God. You feel high in life when you meet all your desires and aims in your life.

These important milestones of happiness come at few times in our ordinary lives. ***These high points in life leave an indelible impact on your balance life.*** When you refer them from your memory, they come without straining any gray cells of your cranium. They come naturally and thinking about them in your down time, uplifts your gloomy mood. These points bring a smile on your lips unknowingly.

Have you had such high points in your life?

I have a few such periods in my life when I felt high. In my entire span of 46 years, a few, which come instantaneously to my mind, are:-

- The day, I scored my first century, in cricket, at my school.
- The day, I passed my services selection board for National Defence Academy. I thought that I had conquered the world.
- The day, my father burdened my shoulders, with my first pips of a Second Lieutenant, on my passing out from Indian Military Academy.
- The day, I got married to my most loving wife.
- The day, my first child was bundled into my arms.

- The day, I took over the command of my Rashtriya Rifles Battalion.
- The day, my unit eliminated the first terrorist under my command.
- The day, the Indian Army pinned a medal on my chest.
- The day, when my first literary work, a military fiction novel, *Crimson Kashmir* was published.

I have led a very ordinary life till date. I will continue to live an ordinary life, like millions before me and millions after me. Life has been sedate if I may be allowed to say so. We ordinary people do not ruffle life. We ordinary people live at the pace dictated by life. We ordinary people live with that genetic defect of living life. **We ordinary people have very few high points in life to cherish.** We let the tide of time and burden of circumstances diminish our desire to celebrate happiness. We ordinary people are woefully superstitious of the fact that courting happiness harbingers woes later.

From my above tabulated high points in life, what I am getting around to will be clearer in a few lines later. I have very few high points in life.

I have only ten high points in life, in the life span of my lived 46 years, which come to me without thinking. To get them right mathematically on the time line of one's life, one high point for every 4.6 years of my life. A very sad state of affairs indeed to live your life. When I asked the similar question to my wife, she could only recount two. A pathetic state of life to live in, where you have one high point in life for each twenty years lived on this earth.

Are we living life or wasting life?

Are you living life or wasting this one precious life? This metaphorical question, can only be answered by you in your full honesty and not by me.

I think that if I am timing one high point in 46 years then I am definitely wasting this one precious life and not living it the way it should be lived.

When this line of thought hit me for the first time in my life, I again perceived myself to be an abject failure. What made a difference between a successful life and a failed one? Who is a man amongst men? Who is that elusive man? Does such a man exist? Who are those successful men? **What do they do differently than ordinary people like me?**

These successful men have more high points in life. They achieve them with regular monotony. By the time the euphoria of one high point in time wears off due to the vagaries of time, they put another high point in place to savour its accomplishment. You will find all such successful men, in all the walks of life, **who achieve a better hit rate of high points in life, on the time line of life**, than ordinary people like you and me.

That day I resolved that I should strive to reduce the high point gap in life. I strove for the self-imposed goal of one high point in life in one year. If I achieved that, I felt the life would be worth living and savouring. Oh what an accumulated success at the end of life, when I am ready to kick the bucket, I will happily ride the Yama's bull, happy in the thought that I achieved fifty high points in life.

When we reduce the time distance between the high points in the life, we achieve a period of constant high life. Thus, we achieve a longer period of happiness.

We should strive for a period of high life.

Do you recount any such period in your life?

I recount mine, my heart says so and so does my wife, and women can seldom be wrong when commenting upon the happy periods of their husbands' life. It was the two and half years of command of my Rashtriya Rifles unit. Whatever, I thought was what a professional soldier should achieve or could achieve or see, I felt, I saw and achieved in that period. I saw orgy of blood. I saw death. I witnessed bravery. I experienced cowardice. I saw sadness. I saw broken spirits. I saw happiness and I saw laughter. The difficult, disastrous or painful times looked so livable. We had our good times, bad times and terrible times. I boast, brag, chest beat, have nostalgia and slur in pegs of my alcoholic induced happiness, when I talk of that period.

This is what high life periods do to you in life.

High periods in life make you immensely happy.

High periods in life give you the confidence to face adversities bravely.

High periods in life make difficult times look so ordinary.

High periods in life make other life's moments worthy of being cherished.

It brings me to one more interesting point. Do we cherish life moments? **Is life only of series of successes and high points?** Is their no other way to attain happiness. **How does a poor man, devoid of all earthly and materialistic wants be happy in life?** Can a villager in remote corner of my country be happy in comparison with things I think make me happy? *How does a penniless naked fakir exhibit more happiness than a successful self-made billionaire who maybe having hundreds of high points to savour in life?*

Do such men have different parameters with what they gauge happiness. I think they do, for here are my observations.

- Have we unknowingly set too high a standard for achieving a high point in life?

- Have we forgotten to be high on simple things of life?
- Does the first ray of new sun bring a high point worth cherishing and thanking your maker for having been granted this unique opportunity to see a new blessed day?
- Is the innocent smile of your child not a high point in your daily life?
- Is not seeing happiness steeped in your wife's face a high point?
- Will you not consider the pride in our mother's eye a high point?

***When we cherish simple things in life,* which we have taken for granted, *we could achieve a continuous high life*. You will achieve what I believe sages call, nirvana.**

Here the Gyan of Vigyan (Yoga), the teachings of universal spirituality, as tabulated in various Godly forms, can come to our aid. But then this is not a book about spirituality, actualisation of self, but about actions and time in this uninteresting world.

My second solution that I offer you is to work on your desires, which help you attain your aim in life.

☆ ☆ ☆

THINGS YOU NEED TO DO

- Identify Your Road Map To Nirvana.
- Identify High Points In Your Life.
- Identify Low Points In Your Life.
- Identify Simple Things You Cherish.

"Time and tide wait for no man."

— Mark Twain

Chapter 4

Time: The Diminishing Constant

Our learned friend on the previous page is partly right. **Time waits for none, though the tide may technically have to wait for the moon.**

When my blossoming mathematically declined son read the heading, he grinned with a knowing understanding and said, "Don't be funny dad. I at least know that a constant is a constant and it cannot diminish."

On that acute observation, my grade tenth son is right. However, when time is applied to life, I may be able to prove just a point I want to make and maybe not be able to topple the mathematical symmetry.

I want to put my thesis forward based on the following facts of life.

You have one life to live.

The day you were born, you were destined to die.

You have one life to achieve your dreams.

Dream urges translate into your desires.

Fulfilling desires helps you to attain your aims in life.

And you have only one life to live.

We get the time constant from the first two facts as narrated above. Any reasonable man can assume to his own ability or if you believe in tarot cards or horoscope to generally know about your life span. In this better world of preventive medicine and better nutrition, we can assume a reasonable life span of seventy-five years. Therefore, the constant life span can be assumed and assigned. Thus, it is your life, the one life of seventy-five years, your time span to achieve your desires.

Seventy-five years is thus constant. Its beginning and end are visible. The distance in-between, the both ends of the spectrum, can be timed. It is not going to increase under any circumstances. It is fixed in time and space. Thus, the time now can be reflected as a constant.

Now let us introduce the diminishing quantity to it and try to prove my theory of diminishing constant. I will introduce only two basic issues for simplicity of your understanding. Sleeping and basic need time. I will also assume your childhood of little consequence in your ability to plan life. A normal healthy body, which I assume you have, you need as per doctors, minimum eight hours of mandatory sleep. I will give you another two hours in a day to eat, dress and meet your toilet routine.

Let us now calculate.

Time available = **75 years.**

To sleep (8 hours/day) = (7*365 days*75/24=9.12 years). Say **9 years**.

Time available: 75–9= **66 years.**

For basic time (2 hours/day) = (2*365*75=2.28 years). Say **2.5 years**.

Time available: 66–2.5 = **63.5 years.**

Time of childhood= **13.5 years.**

Time available= 63.5–13.5= **50 years.**

From the above it is being proved that the constant you assumed to be available for seventy-five years now has diminished to fifty years.

I have not tabulated other aspects of your life, which you indulge on daily basis or happen to your body. Think how the time available to achieve your dreams will diminish if we include, recreational time, commuting time, illness time, socialising time, acquiring higher education time, idle chatter time, etc. Those fifty years of aim achieving time bank, will look horribly wrong.

Fifty years to achieve my aspirations, fulfil my desires, dreams and only one life to live.

We have certain number of desires, say ten to achieve, when I will say quits, for I would have achieved what I wanted to in life. Let us assume them to be ten such desires in numbers which satiate your inner turbulent beats of ego in terms of achievements.

On an elastic timeline of seventy-five years put a mark when those ten identified desires should logically fructify. Then, let the go of that elastic timeline and let it take its natural position, which reflects fifty-year timeline.

The time diminishes with frightful speed.

For each desire not fulfilled, for reasons best known to you, (from your lack of effort or time or unfavourable circumstances) the burden passes down the timeline available.

From your earlier estimate of 7.5 years per desire, it is reduced to 5 years per desire. If we cannot achieve two desires as per the timeline then it will further reduce to 4 years per desire. To retain your sanity, either give up your two of the desires or work now harder to achieve your ten tabulated desires. However, giving up was not an option discussed in achieving full satisfaction of life, well lived, so we have to work that much harder. ***Men who do not work hard are generally classified, in the end of the day, as failures.***

Is it true that all men who work hard in life achieve their life objectives? No, it is not true as a universal rule. It is not how hard you work but how hard you work intelligently. Why do some metal smiths remain metal smiths and some graduate to establishing factories. Why does one diligent hardworking storekeeper remains at same station in life and other graduates to as the manager in the same factory. You need vision along with your hard work and you need to be organised in your work output.

When you are visionless and not focused then failure does beset you despite your hard work.

On the timeline of life achievements when you miss one aim, and the desire to achieve it remains and then you are trapped by the inadequacies of time available, then the frustration accumulates. As the frustration steps in, your ability to resolve your problem or achieve that dream reduces, enabling you to bad-mouth about fleeting time.

This is my very own formula to tabulate the speed of fleeting time. It is not supposed to win any Nobel Prize nor is intended to stun the mathematical world. It is just to kick your sleeping mind awake to the escaping reality of life: the time.

Formula of Speed of Diminishing Time.

The rate or the speed of its diminishing dimension is to the power cube to your expected time on earth.

Rate of diminishing time (called ohs) = Number of unfulfilled desire multiplied by the cube of time elapsed unfruitfully.

Dt = Dn*(Ta– Tf)*3

Where

Dt = Speed of diminishing time (called ohs).

Dn= Total number of unfulfilled desires.

Ta= Total time available.

Tf = Total fruitful time used.

Ohs are the number of heartbeats you miss per day when your desires are not fulfilled. They put additional burden on remaining time.

Let me explain by giving mathematical examples.

Example One. A man has 50 years available. He has not achieved seven desires and has been able to devote ten fruitful years to achieve his life objectives.

Dt= 7(50 – 10)*3 = 448000 ohs.

What the hell I do with ohs. Well we can convert it into the time it will actually represent which you will now have to put in extra to achieve your unfinished targets.

Divide your total ohs with the 24 hours, and then divide again with number of days in a year ie 365 and lastly number of desires fulfilled. Therefore we get 448000/24/365/3= **17 years of additional burden.**

Yes, now I have to work a whopping span of 17 years extra with dedication to make good the loss of earlier fruitful time.

Example Two. A man has 50 years available. He has not achieved seven desires and has been able to devote twenty fruitful years to achieve his life objectives.

Dt= 7(50 – 20)*3 = 189000 ohs.

Additional burden= 189000/24/365/3= **7.2 years.**

Example Three. A man has 50 years available. He has not achieved two desires and has been able to devote twenty fruitful years to achieve his life objectives.

Dt= 2(50 – 20)*3 = 54000 ohs.

Additional burden=54000/24/365/8= **.77 years.**

Eureka, now I feel like a Nobel laureate, for I have mathematically proved that the fleeting rate

of time can be reduced if you increase your fruitful time. You will reduce the basic heartbeats you miss. ***Therefore, to achieve your life targets increase your fruitful time.***

There is another way to reduce your ohs, **reduce your number of desires.**

But path of all ever true and enlightened Buddha or ever practical Gandhi, I do not want to tread on this materialistic world nor is it my suggestion. You will reach your spiritual plane in life, of no desires, at the time of your own choosing. I need not waste my efforts to coax you in that direction. The elusive spirituality will come and it will come at its own time.

So now I can very vocally state that ***in case you have to achieve your stated desires in life, then increase your fruitful time you allocate to achieving your desires and also reduce your number of desires.***

We can also ***reduce the additional burden of time by fulfilling your desires the earliest.***

However, how do you fulfill your desires? I have a very limited reservoir of knowledge to offer any worthwhile assistance. But I am doubly sure that we can never fulfill our desires if we

- *By sitting, idle?*
- *By not organising your life?*
- *By not formulating your desires?*

- *By not formulating your aims in life?*
- *By not assigning fruitful time to your pursuits?*
- *By not working hard?*
- *By not adhering to time management?*

The additional burden on your body and mind can only be reduced by your ability to organising your life and following time schedules that you have set for yourself.

My observations come back a full circle.

- **Time does not wait for anyone.**
- **Time is a constant.**
- **Time is a diminishing commodity.**
- **Time reduces with astonishing speed when desires are left unfulfilled.**
- **Unfulfilled desires leave you grasping for attaining your mission in life: a life well lived and fully accomplished.**
- **You have only one life to live and fulfil your desires.**

My third preaching to you is to allocate fruitful time on your productive desires, which propel you forward towards your aims.

☆ ☆ ☆

THINGS YOU NEED TO DO

- Try To Calculate Your Expected Time On Earth.
- Calculate Your Total Time On Earth.
- Allocate What You Feel Is The Fruitful Time You Can Give To Fulfil Your Desires.

"You are the origin of worlds and you are Time, their destroyer."

— The Mahabharata

CHAPTER 5

Treacherous Time in Treacherous Times

My father used to say, *"**You fool with time, the time will fool around with you.**"* I will even go a step further than those good times when my father must have firmed in his observations. **You fool with time then it will stab you in back** and at the most crucial juncture when you need it the most.

For these are not so good times.

You must be wondering why I am using a expression 'treacherous time'. The fact that ***when you need it the most, it is the least available commodity.*** Felt familiar, with a knowing sinking feeling just before your exams, or prior to a very important office presentation, or when you have to brief your boss pronto and when you are timing leashed time with your girlfriend. You need those extra precious seconds but those elusive additional moments, you are desperately seeking, treacherously, run away at a very stunning speed.

Moreover, the treacherous times are such.

Ask your father about the frivolity of these times. My dad used to go mad at us for wasting our precious time by reading comics, listening to radio, playing any team game or playing junk on record players. We find the same malaise creeping into our children. They are TV addicts, gaming addicts and mall culture addicts. But so was my father when they would run off to a cinema or hanker any elder of the family to narrate the tales of the Vedas etc. The information age has changed the perspective the way our elders and now our children pass the time. From my father's times of **one technological gizmo**, to our times of **three such gizmos**, my child has **eight such marvels of technology** to bang his head on and that too only for pure entertainment. The power of these tools to capture and transform the mind from an adolescent to an adult is amazing.

Therefore, these are treacherous times.

They give you too many options. They rob you of focus when it is needed. You feel incompetent if you do not know about the technological gadgets. They are adrenalin. They cloud your vision to other realities of life. **They cloud your vision.** They rob you of other rational reason. They make you self-effusing and self-indulgent. They most importantly eat your precious time. My son would rather play video game than to meet his friends. He would watch television to calm down from any perceived agitation of mind. Information creepers have started controlling your mind and body functions. You have left the reality and simplicity of life behind and aside.

The technology is making the times treacherous.

Treacherous time and the treacherous times are interlinked and woven into the fabric of each other. The common thread, which binds them, strangely, is not the galloping technology, but the time itself.

The time has been stolen out of your life.

- **One life to live and so many things to experience.**
- **One life to live and so many things to do.**
- **One life to live and so many lives to live.**
- **So many lives to live for so many things to do.**
- **So many things to do and only one life to live.**

Where the hell or heaven is the time.

Hey, guys do not fret. The world is not going to come tumbling down for I have a solution for a change. ***The time is right in your hands.*** I am not joking and military people never ever have a funny bone by their side. Their selection process is so much skewed to let any funny bone hang by their side. So, believe me when I say, the time is always by your side.

Plenty of time is available.

It is right besides your heart. It lies in your mind. It rests in your body. It rubs on in plenty on your palms. It is within the perception of your vision. It harbours deep inside the cornea of your eyes.

Time is in plenty but problem is only one.

We just cannot find it. Where is the time?

So many things to do and only one life to live and you say there is plenty of time.

Yes, the time is in plenty. It is available for taking, as much as you want. Just only, search for it. You may not even do that, please just open the closed portals of your heart or open the inner eye of your brain, to see it, it being wasted in plenty.

Who in his sane mind will waste time when time is such a rare commodity? These are not so good times and they are treacherous and time cannot be wasted in these times, for life is one, to achieve my dreams.

Who in his sane mind will waste time when time is such a precious commodity? Certainly not a military moustache plucker like me and certainly not you, a saner person, based on a very simple premise, for the saner choice of profession you keep.

Then, if we are sure, that we are sane and not wasting time in these treacherous times then are we utilising the time properly so it does not behave treacherously?

Are we absolutely sure?

We are very conscious. We do not take a nap at work. We do not indulge in idle chatter. We only take authorised breaks at work. We do not daydream. We are focused on job at hand. We party for the sake of party once a month. We keep our relationship lines with our bosses, juniors, wives, kids, parents and friends open twenty-four hours. We do not snooze, laze or be late. We are prompt. We are punctual to a tee. We foresee problems and take corrective steps. My car is always working, pens inked, pencils sharpened. Batteries of all my essential gadgets are in place, and eureka, I keep spares too. We plan ahead. We plan for the day. We plan for the month and definitely for the year. No we plan our life too.

Yes, we are absolutely sure, that, in these treacherous times, we do not waste any precious time.

I do not mix business with pleasure. I only eat to sustain my body. I keep my desk clean of pending files. I am ready with the assigned paperwork/ presentations one day ahead of time. I am never late for my child's birthday or my mother's for one. My engagement pads are updated and I keep all my prior engagements. I am very organised. My children and peers ape me for the goodness of it. I am there always to help my wife whenever she needs me. I keep a lot of spare time up my sleeve due to the efficiency I display at work. I move ahead of time always.

Do you?

I learnt it a very hard way the concept of one life.

The evening was fast converting into the evil of darkness, in a remote corner of Lolab Valley in Kashmir. I was deploying with my buddy for an ambush on a suspected terrorist taken path. Five meters apart, both facing outside to cover each other's back, I had just settled in. Suddenly, from behind my back, my buddy opened fire and within seconds I heard the whine of bullets knock my eardrums off. It must have taken me less than a second to realise that the encounter, with the terrorists, had started behind me and then less than a second to roll back to take cover from my exposed back. ***In that less than a second, my life flashed by.*** From my earliest memories, good or bad, to the present time, in one flash the life passed by. Its entire existence of forty-two years summed up in less than a second. I lost by buddy that night to the terrorists but not before he had shot down two.

One life.

One life for my buddy and another life to live for me.

And that night I realised how much I loved the concept of life and it rhymed with my favourite cliché, ***"You have never lived unless you have almost died."***

And that day I realised I had so many things to do in life and maybe rising high in my career was just one of many such desires. My aims and objectives in life and of life changed dramatically in that flash of a second. Suddenly, I had a big wish list of desires.

- Desire to be a very high ranking officer was replaced by an equally strong desire to do something equally more meaningful in life.
- I desired to be an author of at least one fiction novel.
- I desired to know foxtrot and tango. I desired to learn to play music.

- I desired to go on a world cruise in a luxury ocean liner.
- I desired to present a rare diamond solitaire to my wife.
- I desired to uplift my family from the perceived cycle of materialistic poverty.
- I desired to buy my mother a penthouse.
- I desired to learn, gain knowledge, be useful, and be a good man.

One life and so many things to do.

We are efficient and we do not waste time.

We foresee ahead and plan ahead.

We foresee our desires and plan ahead to fulfil those desires.

We can achieve most of our stated desires and the mantra is very simple. Allocate in a day fruitful time for each of your desires. Nevertheless, in these treacherous times where is the time? Yes, there is plenty of time once you eliminate the treacherous time. **Eliminate all your time wasters. Eliminate time, which offers no value.** If you savour the taste of wild berries and it gives you immense satisfaction, then by all means, allocate six hours a day to eating wild berries. Allocate time for your each desire. Allocate time for your goals. Allocate time for your long and short-term aims in life.

Once you do that, one step at a time, one small push at a time, one dream at a time, one page or a paragraph at a time, you would have begun a journey, which has no previous stops. How the mighty is conquered, you would not even come to fathom.

My fourth advice to you is to focus on the time available at hand to complete your objectives in life.

☆ ☆ ☆

THINGS YOU NEED TO DO

- Identify When In Your Life You Felt That The Time Was Treacherous.
- Identify Your Time Wasters In These Treacherous Times.
- Allocate Time To Your Desires On Daily, Weekly, Monthly And Yearly Basis.

"Time present and time past,
Are both perhaps present in time future.
And time future contained in the time past.
All time is eternally present."

— Elliot

Chapter 6

Taming Time

Have you ever tamed anything in life?

Most probably not.

Taming is most demanding word in English dictionary. It is about the turbulence. It is about control. It is about patience. It is about fatigue. It is about anger. It is about curbing your instincts. It is about killing your heart for that moment. It is about sweat, toil and tears. It is about being jeered at. It is about doing something different. It is about being in the state of antitheses to your known ways of natural existence. It is about learning a new way to exist. It is about hard senseless training.

Have you ever witnessed a wild horse being tamed?

Did you notice how he fights for his freedom, his way of burdenless, carefree life? He whines and neighs. He jumps, twists, rolls and cries fowl at every step. He bites into his bridle, pulls at that confounding restraining rope. He uses every guile he knows in his armoury to throw the rider off. The wild horse fights for his known way of life.

Have you ever witnessed any cocaine addict trying to tame his addiction?

He cramps, convulses, vomits, goes breathless, sweats, howls, whimpers, bleeds against his restraining shackles, kicks, screams, begs, shivers, soils and is shameless.

Both the horse and the addict ultimately get tamed and live in that state of tamed existence, till they decide to get tamed again. On and off, the twitch to lead that earlier vagabond existence returns. They get tamed but with lesser effort this time.

But how does one tame that is eternally present, like time, like free thoughts or like freedom.

If you think that, you have the ability to tame time, without any efforts on your part, I think you are living in a fool's paradise. Men of spirituality, men who dedicated their whole lives to Vigyan of yoga could barely touch the time and claim that they had tamed it. Gods who have attained immortality have, but we are not gods, but poor human beings. Nevertheless, at best with available wherewithal, we can at least try.

Time as such is an elusive commodity in such treacherous times. It is not in your hands to tame time. It is not a thing you can hold in your hands and twist about. It is not a living being you can woo or talk too. **Time is an illusion. Time is a distant mirage. Time can never be perceived in forms of matter**. You cannot train time. Your plethora of worldly gods cannot train or tame time.

Period.

Time cannot be trained hence it cannot be tamed.

To get back at time, to have always plentiful of time in these treacherous times and to always remain ahead of the elusive time, I think that I do know a way. However, my thoughts are very mundane, very simple and so doable that, I muster adequate courage, to show my fellow compatriots, the way.

- **To tame time, tame yourself.**
- **To tame time, tame your unproductive desires.**

- **To tame time, train yourself to tame yourself.**
- **To tame time, train yourself to expel the time wasters from your life.**

Moreover, how does one train himself to tame the time in such treacherous times. There are so many imponderables. So many brain catchers, so many aim evaders, so many effusive satisfaction providers, so many sinful things to indulge in and so many other things to experience, which take you off your life's road map.

Training, like any training, whether be mind or physical, has never been easy. ***But train you must to tame time.*** Train you must to have time in your grasp in bountiful measure. Train you must to remain ahead of time always and every time.

When you train, you actually tame yourself. It is a conditioned reflex. It is that unquestionable obedience to command. It is that brainless regimentation. ***It is that character you wish to mould.*** It is combining all those to make it a habit.

Habits are conditioned traits. We love them in the military. Without such conditioned traits, we would not have an obedient army. One word of command, thousands turn right. One battle cry, thousands charge the enemy.

We, when I say we, I mean most of sane society, and not those lunatics living on the edge of it, do get conditioned to do something good. Your parents taught to brush first thing in the morning. You pray at regular intervals. You eat three meals a day. You sleep at night. These are simple manifestations of your conditioned reflex response how you deal with your daily routine. These are good conditioned traits, which become good habits, to make you a good human being.

In addition, to achieve the good you have aimed for in life, will you not train to ingrain a good conditioned trait and make another good habit?

Training is essential to tame time and training is needed to tame time.

What should one train in to tame time. My list is endless. Its course, I dare say, is not available in any university in the world. It cannot be taught, to humanity, in classrooms of wisdom. The course cannot be straightjacketed for two twin brothers leave alone a class. It cannot be taught in classes, for the basic fact of the matter is that it is very individualistic in nature, the contents of that training capsule. It varies extremely from man to man. Some grasp the essentials in seconds and some take a lifetime of tries and still be elusive to its goodness. For some it comes very early in life and for some very late. For me it came around less than the middle part of my life and I thank my God for it.

However, the list, to train in what we need to do, is endless.

We need to have aims in life.

We need to have long-term aim of ultimate nirvana and several short-term aims, which are visible in a horizon, to keep us motivated to help us reach that state of nirvana.

We need to have productive desires, which help us to achieve aims in our lives.

We need to eliminate negative unproductive desires.

We need to identify all the time wasters, which keep us off the path of life of our fulfillment.

We need to allocate small bits of time to work on each desire.

We need to plan ahead, foresee problems and find workable solutions.

We need to be attentive, be efficient and play with efficient tools backing our work.

We need to allocate time as an investment in our life.

We need to accomplish all in this one life.

We need to be focused in life.

We need to guard from these treacherous times.

I will just give a simple example how I confronted efficiency for first time in my life. I learnt it astonishingly from my happy go lucky wife.

She would get up and hit the kitchen by 0615 in the morning and by the time I came to the breakfast table and later my children, her two meals for the day were cooked and she serving us hot steaming breakfast. I would always quip what is the hurry bun. Prompt would come the reply, I get time at my hand to do other things. Now, what other things they were, was her choice, which was to read ten thousand books of Mills and Boons in her lifetime. She seems to fulfilling her childhood desire of endless romantic streak in life. If that is her aim in life, it is perfectly fine. She saved time but by sheer prior planning. Her lentils would be soaked a day prior, her vegetables chopped earlier and her basic ingredients in place one night before. ***Therefore, you need to plan to save time thus tame time.***

I have not said anything stumping, novo, original or wisdom dawning.

Read any book of Gods or a Yale management guru, they will spell them same, maybe worded a little differently and maybe a wee bit in different pecking order.

My fifth mantra is as simple as the previous ones, ***'Train yourself to tame time'.***

☆ ☆ ☆

THINGS YOU NEED TO DO

- Identify Your Road Map To Nirvana.
- Identify Your Inefficiencies, Which Inhibit From Reaching Ladders Of Excellence.
- Allocate Time In Training Yourself In Overcoming Your Inefficiencies.
- Identify How You Will Utilise Time As An Investment Tool In Enhancing Your Life Objectives.

"Time stays long enough for everyone who will use it."

— Leonardo Da Vinci

CHAPTER

7

Time Trap

Time trap is as good as any trap, which can be defined. One finds oneself lured into it innocently or stupid - walk right into it with eyes open in a snare of time. We know it is there but close our functional brain of avoiding it.

It is akin to taming time. It is taming time for it is the exact antithesis of it. If we do not tame time, we walk into time trap and find no solution to come out winning.

Have you had the honour of experiencing the feeling of being trapped in a situation?

Have you ever smelled your fear when a situation goes horribly wrong around you?

How did you feel when you were last trapped?

Heartbeat pound in a furious pace, vision dims up to a perception limit of few feet, you want to bolt out in utter panic, your mouth turns Sahara dry, your bowls become acutely loose and few with lesser constitution would wet their underpants willingly and the confounding situation never seems to end.

I have smelt fear in very tiring circumstances. I am sorry if my circumstance is just not the ordinary one, which millions compare by but then our service situations are not for the ordinary. I was leading six teams into thick jungles for a raid on suspected terrorist hideout. All was going as per the plan but what we had not planned was the terrorists' reaction in all its eventualities. To cut the story short, after surrounding the terrorists inside the jungles, we found ourselves surrounded. We found ourselves trapped. We were trapped for six hours, a situation; I would never want to be in again my entire life. We eliminated two terrorists, one of our soldiers was critically wounded, but we fought our way out.

How did we do it?

We got better of a situation due to our professionalism, having faith in our abilities, for having prepared for such situations, for displaying courage under fire, for caring for each other, for having done our homework and for having conquered our fears. We got better of the situation for foreseeing before the adversary what was the next thing he could do and do it before him and more importantly utilising the fleeting time to our advantage.

What are the time traps in your life? I gave you just one extreme example.

Have you felt trapped in three hours of an exam? Ever been trapped in a presentation. Ever been trapped in a situation of not your liking?

You feel basically trapped when you are not prepared adequately to handle that situation.

You can also feel trapped when you are prepared more than adequately for the situation, when the time limits are defined.

I will give an example, say of an exam. If you walked in without adequate preparation, you feel lost to a point and wish why those three hours do not finish earlier. **You are trapped for lack of knowledge**. Conversely, when you are more than prepared, you feel the pressure of time for it inhibits you from displaying your entire breadth of knowledge. **You are trapped in excess of**

knowledge. In both the situations, you will emerge as a failure.

Time trapped by the company you keep. Yes, almost all humans are trapped in social bindings. A happy or unhappy marriage. Good or bad friends. Helpful or resentful colleagues. Caring or uncaring boss. We will take only one example of friends. How many friends have you made after school or college? Generally, we are trapped in social bindings, which are twenty years old, those that blossomed in schools, colleges and training institutions. Look around and tell from your heart how many friends you made after your marriage or joining your profession. If the list is smaller than that of pre job days, we have wasted our social opportunities. It is generally the case. We generally are trapped in social bindings of old and **are afraid to explore new horizons.**

Unless you do not make new friends, **you will always be trapped in time twenty years old.**

Unless you do not make new inroads into managing your **time you will always be time trapped in your old habits.** And habits are what you have formed over a period of time by conditioning your body and mind. **Recondition your body and mind to form better habits.**

If one thing has not worked for you do not be afraid to try something new.

You are also **trapped in time due to your physical inabilities, knowledge deficiency and mental development.** As I said earlier that it is not possible for a two-year old to drive an automobile. It is his physical inability to do so. Even if you are thirty years old, you cannot fly a spacecraft, for you are not trained for it, it becomes your knowledge deficiency. At age of twenty, you will find it hard to organise an army or command old generals for your compatible mental faculties are not fully developed. The above factors are sure big inhibitors in achieving your desires but again are not insurmountable. You can do it, provided temper your desires with maturity of age and right time.

In old Hindu philosophy of living life, the level of mental and physical development had been related with time. There was a time to learn. There was a time to start and indulge in a family. There was a time to progress in life. There was a time to renounce the world and live a life of an ascetic. I am not debating the goodness or the badness of the concept, but am trying to highlight only one aspect, **that there is a right time to do a thing.** *That right time you have to find in you.*

However, some men have the exact knack of timing the time to its maximum advantage. These **people win**, score high marks, and give fabulous presentations, **for they practise** or have it ingrained in their psyche, **the art of managing time effectively.** In addition, they are knowledgeable, focused, know the value of time and know how to time the time effectively.

When Emerson said, **"To fill the hour – that is happiness,"** he was not wrong. We can only fill the hour if we beat the time trap. *When we fill that hour, we will attain happiness.*

Formula for Beating Time Trap.

Tt = 2.5Ta/ E*Ft*F

Where

Tt is the time trap and is deemed to be broken if the value comes below one. It represents the ratio of time needed to complete the task and worth put in.

Ta is the total time available to perform a task in minutes.

E is the total effort put at a six-point scale of 1, 1.05, 1.1, 1.15, 1.2 and 1.25.

Ft is the total fruitful time allocated by you in minutes.

F is the focus with you worked at a six-point scale of 1, 1.05, 1.1, 1.15, 1.2 and 1.25.

Example One

If you have a three hour exam and you allocated two fruitful hours to it and gave your best focus and effort.

Then to beat the time trap let us calculate

2.5*180/1.25*120*1.25=450/187.5= 2.4

You are in the time trap.

Example Two

With everything same, we increase the fruitful time to four hours. Then we get

2.5*180/1.25*240*1.25= 450/375= 1.2

You are in the time trap.

Example Three

With everything same, we increase the fruitful time to five hours. Then we get

2.5*180/1.25*300*1.25= 450/468.75= .96

You have just managed to break the time trap.

Now it is evident that to break the time trap we either increase the fruitful time or optimise our effort and focus. Now even if you allocate fruitful time but do not optimise your effort and focus then we never in logical timeframe beat the time trap.

Therefore, to optimise your effort, you have to:-

- Allocate fruitful time to your endeavours.
- You have to be focused on your endeavours.
- You have to allocate effort for your endeavours.

Without any of the above three, I will lay any bet that you will never be able to achieve what you want to achieve in life.

My sixth line of wisdom for you is to explore the avenues, which give you abundance of time to work on your desires.

THINGS YOU NEED TO DO

- Identify Your Time Traps.
- Identify Your Reactions To A Time Trap.
- Identify Your Resources Needed To Beat The Time Trap.
- Identify Time Needed To Amplify Your Time Trap Beating Resources.

"This is not the end,
It is not even the beginning of the end.
But, it is, perhaps,
The end of the beginning."

— Winston Churchill

CHAPTER 8

Timing Time

"If you can fill the unforgiving minute,

With sixty seconds worth of distance run."

I somehow always come back to this verse in Rudyard Kipling's poem written to motivate his son.

One part is the **unforgiving minute.**

Second part is the **worth you run that distance with.**

Time is very unforgiving. It goes ahead every second and does not come back. Time once wasted cannot be recovered by normal application of energy. You have to slog double to catch up with it.

If the distance requires sixty seconds to run to achieve the optimum, then sixty-second worth of distance must be run. *Not a second more or a second less.*

One second less will let you achieve the target but you would have *wasted your extra energy*. Conversely, *one second extra* will *not get* you to *your objective*. That extra energy you wasted and extra second you again wasted could have been channelled to achieve something more useful. ***Time is a very precious commodity***. We cannot play or fool around with it. **Time gone cannot come back** despite Jules Verne trying to zoom his flying machine back into time.

But endless examples are with us that despite giving your worth the targets remain elusive. They generally do remain elusive for the simple reason that our worth was a very worthy effort on our part but was not handled well.

Let me clarify the issue with an example.

An expert metal smith puts in exact worth of heat into hard metal to soften its core. Not a degree less or a degree more of heat is needed as it will either not soften the metal or melt it uselessly. He times his stroke to perfection, not a second earlier or a second later, to give that applied worth through his hammer to mould the unyielding iron into his desired objective. Any deviation from his timing the stroke will result in extra or wasted effort.

Therefore, it becomes paramount that ***we learn to time our time intelligently.*** Our worth should not be wasted due to mistiming of time.

Therefore, it is important that we, along with putting in the required worth, ***master the art of timing the right stroke at right time.*** Boat racing is an apt example of the same. All put in their worth in their oars, and that boat finishes first, where the worth was applied with synchronised timing of oars. The oar synchronised boat skims through the water with minimum ripples. ***When you time the time perfectly or to the optimum, you do not leave the ripples of wastage behind.***

In your daily routine, do you leave ripples of your incompetence behind?

We, over the various chapters, have established the **following facts.**

- We have one life to live as we have one life to achieve.
- Time is a diminishing constant.
- We need to have our aims and desires in place.
- We need to allocate fruitful time to our aims and desires.

- Fruitful time is a rare precious commodity.
- We need to embrace high life.
- In order to succeed, we need to be ahead of time.
- To have additional time in our hands, we need to tame time.
- We can tame time provided we dispel our inefficiencies.
- Efficiency enables us to beat time traps.
- Once we overcome our time traps, we can devote additional time fruitfully.
- Additional fruitful time enables us to reach high points in life with lesser time gaps.

To fathom your ripples of incompetence you need to know what you do in your daily routine. In earlier chapters, you had calculated total time available to you to fulfill your desires. You had allocated fruitful time for pursuance of those aims and desires. **Have you ever tabulated your daily routine?** I want you to do an exercise, which I am sure will not take more than ten minutes of your time. Let us tabulate in spectrum of time, your activities of the day as mentioned below. Fill value of **actual time spent** ahead of each column until you reach the figure of 24 hours.

- Sleeping.
    - At night.

  - In afternoon.
  - Power nap in office.
- Eating/Drinking (at home and office).
  - Breakfast.
  - Lunch.
  - Dinner.
  - Supper.
  - Tea/Coffee.
  - Snacks.
  - Drinking.
- Social Interaction With.
  - Wife.
  - Children.
  - Parents.
  - Colleagues.
  - Seniors.
  - Juniors.
  - Friends.
- Physical Exercise/Walking.
  - At home.
  - At office.

- Meditation.
  - At home.
  - At office.
- Computer (Not related to work).
  - At home.
  - At office.
- Computer (Related to work).
  - At home.
  - At office.
- Telephone (not work).
  - At home.
  - At office.
- Telephone (work).
  - At home.
  - At office.
- Relaxation.
  - At home.
  - At office.
- Entertainment.
  - At home.
  - At office.

- Idle/Gossip.
  - At home.
  - At office.
- Commuting.
  - At home.
  - For office.
  - For official engagements.
- Passing Orders.
  - At home.
  - At office.
- Supervision (work).
  - At home.
  - At office.
- Work (Your Job).
  - At home.
  - At office.
- To Your Life Aim.
  - At home.
  - At office.
- To Your Present Desire.
  - At home.
  - At office.
- Total Time.

At the end of my very own exercise, in allocating my most precious commodity, time, I was the most embarrassed man on this side of Suez Canal. Please do not ask for my actual result, I feel very inhibited to give it, but let me give you glimpses of my daily routine time profile.

I spent a lifetime commuting. I went from one place to another where a silly phone or a sensible letter could have had the same effect. For most of the commuting time, I slept or wandered in useless thoughts.

I indulged shamelessly in my favourite pastime of gluttony. Every other hour I was eating or drinking something. My acute tummy is a mute testimony to the same.

I do not want to be equated with other fifty percent of human race known for and having a penchant for gossip. Idle was I many a time a day.

I did take care of my health and mind. I meditated, did my yoga and went for long morning walks. Still it does no justice to my supportive paunch and my impatience with my children. Did I give my actual worth or was I poodle faking. I think I have the answer.

I did almost everything than to devote adequate time to my family.

I did almost everything than to actually work.

I did almost everything than to focus on my aims and desires of my life.

With such an enviable track record of my daily routine and time management and compatible results achieved, do I have the courage to say that I have left no ripples of my incompetence behind. Maybe, I never had the courage to look behind.

If I had not left ripples of my incompetence behind, then my boss should always be happy with me. Let me assure you he is not. Is my wife happy? On scale of ten, she reflects her happiness pegged at four in her ultimate bliss with me. How incongruous to the fact that I love her as the most precious gift in my life. My children say I am grumpy and grouchy. My mother says I just do not care for her troubles. My friends think that I am high headed. My schedules are not topsy-turvy but not perfect either. In paper work, I do miss a few important letters at least once a quarter. In my own eyes, my aims are being met but not with the consistency of a one high point a year. Once in four years yes.

Am I progressing satisfactorily in life?

Is my life so organised?

Am I so organised?

Am I timing my time optimally?

Does one day of my life runs like a well-oiled machine? If it does not then I certainly need to open my mind to new frontiers of managing time.

Formula for Timing Time.

Tim t = Tt / N o

Tim t is timing the time to your advantage and the time is deemed tamed to your advantage if its value comes below one.

Tt is the ability to break the time trap as learnt in the earlier chapter.

N o is the number of objectives, aims or tasks you have completed. ie (N o1 + N o2).

Basically the formula represents the ratio of time efficiency where the input (total effort put) are divided by output (number of objectives achieved). It is opposite of basic formula of efficiency of output over input.

Example One

You have fulfilled one task and your time trap worked out at 1.2. Then we have:-

1.2/1= 1.2 thus you have not tamed the time.

Example Two

You have fulfilled one task and your time trap worked out at .97. Then we have:-

.97/1= .97 thus you have tamed the time to you advantage.

What we learn is that to time the time perfectly (i.e. is to optimise time to maximum) in relation with desired output we have to learn to beat the time trap effectively.

My seventh solution for you is to learn to identify the importance of fleeting time, by optimising its availability.

☆ ☆ ☆

THINGS YOU NEED TO DO

- Identify How You Spend Your Time Daily.
- Identify Ripples Of Your Incompetence.
- Identify How You Will Synchronise Your Time With Worth Put.

"Time shall unfold what
plighted cunning hides,
Who cover faults, at
last shame them derides."

— William Shakespeare
(King Lear)

Chapter 9

Fudging Time

When you fudge anything in life, life fudges your dreams. You can succeed by fudging, twice or thrice may be at times ten. One generally fails and fails so badly that it is difficult to honourably get up and brush the dust off one's pants.

Then here I am suggesting you to fudge time. I must be off my rocker. Nevertheless, believe me, I am not quiet insane as my proposal is.

We fudge the time intelligently. We fudge the time to beat its time trap. We fudge the time to tame it better. We fudge the time to ensure we remain ahead on the time always and every time. We fudge the time to ensure that we always have plenty of it on our hands. We fudge time to ensure we reduce the burden of additional time we need to achieve our life objectives.

We fudge the time by applying an efficiency constant to it.

Efficiency constant?

If we are efficient we save time. Efficiency does not come naturally. One has to train for it. It is very attainable. Once you train for it, it becomes your body armour, a habit, which is hard to shake off. People who seem to have endless time are just more efficient and thus save time to employ it to other pursuits.

Here I will not be very off the mark to offer a quote by Jackson Brown,

"Don't say you do not have time. You have exactly the same number of hours per day that were given to Helen Keller, Pasteur, Michelangelo, Mother Teresa, Leonardo Da Vinci, Thomas Jefferson and Albert Einstein ."

Let us strive to do what they could achieve in life, not in their achievements, but let us emulate their good habits. Let us strive to be efficient.

I have my very own little **efficiency constant**. I have pegged it at .8 for I feel that one can easily save up to twenty percent of one's time by just being more organised and being efficient. Imagine additional four hours and forty-eight minutes in a day of twenty-four hours.

Now let us apply our efficiency constant to our earlier discovered formulas on time and fudge formulas of the time silly.

Formula of Speed of Diminishing Time.

The rate or the speed of its diminishing dimension is to the power cube to your expected time on earth.

Rate of diminishing time (called ohs) = Number of unfulfilled desire multiplied by the cube of time elapsed unfruitfully.

Dt = [Dn*(Ta– Tf)*3]*e

Where

Dt = Speed of diminishing time (called ohs).

Dn = Total number of unfulfilled desires.

Ta = Total time available.

Tf = Total fruitful time used.

Ohs are the number of heartbeats you miss per day when your desires are not fulfilled. They put additional burden on remaining time.

e = The efficiency constant of .8.

Let me explain by giving mathematical examples.

Example One. A man has 50 years available. He has not achieved seven desires and has been able to devote ten fruitful years to achieve his life objectives.

Dt = 7(50 – 10)*3 = 448000 ohs.

With efficiency constant applied = 448000*.8 = 358400 ohs.

Therefore we get 358400/24/365/3 = **13.6 years of additional burden.**

Definitely better than **17 years of additional burden** (448000/24/365/3) before the application of efficiency constant.

Example Two. Man has 50 years available. Has not achieved two desires and has been able to devote twenty fruitful years to achieve his life objectives.

Dt= 2(50 – 20)*3 = 54000 ohs.

After applying efficiency constant 54000*.8 = 43200 ohs.

Thus we get the additional burden of 43200/24/365/2 = **2.4 years.**

Definitely better than the additional burden of **3 .1 years** before applying efficiency constant.

Formula For Beating Time Trap.

Tt = [2.5Ta/ E*Ft*F]*e

Where

Tt is the time trap and is deemed to be broken if the value comes below one. It represents the ratio of time needed to complete the task and worth put in.

Ta is the total time available to perform a task in minutes.

E is the total effort put at a six-point scale of 1, 1.05, 1.1, 1.15, 1.2 and 1.25.

Ft is the total fruitful time allocated by you in minutes.

F is the focus with you worked at a six-point scale of 1, 1.05, 1.1, 1.15, 1.2 and 1.25.

e is the efficiency constant.

Example One

If you have a three hour exam and you allocated two fruitful hours to it and gave your best focus and effort.

Then to beat the time trap let us calculate

2.5*180/1.25*120*1.25=450/187.5= 2.4

You are in the time trap and you would be in a little lesser time trap had we applied the efficiency constant. Then we would have got 2.4*.8 = **1.92.**

Example Two

With everything same, we increase the fruitful time to four hours. Then we get

2.5*180/1.25*240*1.25= 450/375= 1.2

You are in the time trap and after applying the efficiency constant; we can break the time trap by 1.2*.8 = **.96.**

Formula For Timing Time.

Tim t = [Tt / N o]*e

Tim t is timing the time to your advantage and the time is deemed tamed to your advantage if its value comes below one.

Tt is the ability to break the time trap as learnt in the earlier chapter.

N o is the number of objectives, aims or tasks you have completed. ie (N o1 + N o2).

e is the efficiency constant.

Example

You have fulfilled one task and your time trap worked out at 1.2. Then we have,

1.2/1= 1.2 thus you have not tamed the time but after application of efficiency constant we get 1.2*.8 = **.96** and you have broken the time trap.

It is evident from the above that we can fudge the time by applying the efficiency constant. The absolute value is my very own, after having observed over the period of time efficient and inefficient people around me. Efficient people seldom seemed if they worked for they would have already finished their work and be utilising the saved time on the pursuits they cherished.

My eight mantra for you is, let us be efficient, to save time.

☆ ☆ ☆

THINGS YOU NEED TO DO

- Observe An Efficient Colleague And Tabulate How Much Earlier He/She Completes Task Than The Inefficient One.
- Tabulate Habits Which Will Help You To Be More Efficient.

"The strongest of all warriors
are these two,
Time and Patience."

— Leo Tolstoy
(War and Peace)

CHAPTER 10

Embracing Efficiency

Again, what I am going to throw at you is not stumping. It has been said before. It has been practised before. Such concepts have existed over a period of time. I only offer you the glimpse again, to refresh your thoughts and help you to attain efficiency to organise your life a little better.

Here are a few tips, if you wish to at least retain, twenty percent edge in managing your time. Twenty is my ball mark; yours could be thirty or more. However, one thing is certain, you will not get even one percent, if you do not follow what is being requested of you in paragraphs below.

Scan Read. Learn the art of scan reading. I believe John F Kennedy could scan read a page in fifteen seconds and retain above eighty percent of the key components. *It is good to read in between the lines for important documents but not routine.* It saves a lot of time and you can achieve it, you just need to practise the art.

Avoid Routine. If you have reached a comfortable position, you must relegate routine to lower echelons of your office. It is surprising that eighty percent of the work in any office is routine. *If you have to think innovative, strive for that elusive extra, then try to avoid routine.* Check routine for effectiveness and correctness once in a while and not daily.

Delegate. Learn the art of delegation. We are generally afraid to delegate, trying to keep the full control in our hands. You can never control everything tightly. Situations are fleeting like loose sand. *Try to hold fine dry sand tightly in your hand. You will hold little. Try to hold the loose sand with loose hands; you will hold the maximum sand.* Delegate with full confidence in your subordinates. They will rarely disappoint you. The day they disappoint you then have the moral fibre to stand and accept the mistake as your own.

Tape Thoughts. Good thoughts or those great ideas, which can take you one step towards the

Nobel Prize flash by, when you are the least prepared. Try to tape them on a tape or scribble them on a piece of paper for reference later. It saves time to think about them with clarity afterwards.

Plan Day Daily. Learn to plan the day daily. The exercise you must build in your daily routine and it takes less than a minute a day. Best do it a day before going to bed or early in the morning. Take a piece of paper or your engagement pad and pen down what you want to do in a day. *It will help you to organise the day better and help you to see through the problems of scheduling and thus save time.*

Take Decisions. I knew one officer who would get very angry with his battle mate, especially in the morning, if he were asked how you would like your egg at breakfast. The officer would get very agitated and shout back, "Why do you burden my mind to give a rational decision so early in the day." *Giving decisions can be burdensome for the most.* In the same breath, let me give you the wisdom I imbibed from another officer I met. He said, give a decision instantaneously, for that is what all are looking for. Fifty percent of the time, the decision will be correct and you will be applauded for it. Fifty percent of the time, it will be wrong and out of that fifty percent, the bad decision will be retractable and can be recalibrated and you will again be applauded. For the balance, twenty-five percent, just have the heart to face the stick. *Never ponder over a decision, give it.*

Speed Spell. Learn to write fast. Take away frills of frivolous curves from your writing as they slow you down. I am not suggesting a doctor's scribble but the need to write neater and quicker. Learn short hand, which saves time. *It enables you to pen your ideas with the speed of your thoughts.*

Mind Your Mind. *All the games of life start here and end here.* You need to mind how your mind works. If it is open to new ideas, transparent in clarity of thought and is satisfied, you are on right track. You need to do the following to keep it sharper.

- ***Do not play mind games with your subordinates***. They have little capacity to guess what you desire of them. Tell them what to do.
- ***Focus your thoughts*** *once a day on tasks at hand.* This will enable to clear any cobwebs lingering.
- ***Learn to meditate*** *to enable you to control your agitating mind and allow you to manage better the ability to concentrate thoughts*. Five minutes of apt concentration on a draft is ten times better than thinking about it for an hour.
- ***Retain Clarity of Thoughts***. Muddled mind of the boss is the most irritating aspect to digest. Clarity helps you to see through the problem. Once bigger picture is fixed, you concentrate on smaller issues, which complete the picture.

'Mona Lisa' was created each stroke at a time and not in one go.

- ***Exercise it.*** You need to keep it exercised for rejuvenation. Play cross word, sukudo, scrabble, etc to keep it sharp.
- ***Keep it Positive.*** Your negative thoughts reflect on your irritable actions. Retain positive thoughts for happiness. Happiness brings in more happiness.
- **Discipline** your mind to reduce its emotional gyrations.

Healthy Health. ***Negative health is undue down time,*** which cuts into your already precious time availability. Healthy body is attainable and we all know it. Keep up the following.

- ***Manage Your Anger.*** Remove it from your body and mind as a cancerous ulcer. *It creates negative aura around your personality.* You loose the sanity of reasoning rationally. You waste time overcoming it. You loose precious time thinking un-good. My father used to say, *"Only dogs fight, humans resolve differences".*
- ***Yen for Yoga.*** Learn the art of controlling your mind and body through yoga. Rejuvenate your soul with the help of it. Many disciplines are available to pick the one you require. Make it a routine in your life.
- ***Exercise Daily.*** Apart from yoga, you need to exercise daily to energise your muscles for

retaining muscular vitality. Go for walks, jogs and play sports. It enables you to take out the bad blood in your system by pumping new.

- *Reduce Desires.* Reduce your basic cravings and trappings for what you feel is the good life. It will reduce your burden and anxiety on you mind and heart.

Organise Your Work Station. One peep into my briefcase will tell you in what mess I live in. It takes me more than a minute to find a chequebook or any precious paper I needed for back reference.

- *Use Efficient Tools.* Need I tell you the importance of an ink filled pen, sharpened pencil, eraser or keeping your instruments oiled?
- *Use Technology* to speed up your analysis, for acquiring knowledge, storage of data, its retrieval and communication for saving time.
- *Remove Clutter* from your worktable. Keep it clean of old reports, papers etc which distract you without giving any advantage.
- *Keep your appointments* and never miss them and other dead lines unless you are dead as a dodo.

Clarity of Speech. *With words, we govern men.* So use your words with care. Use them in a manner that they leave no other afterthoughts. They should impart clarity of your line of thought and decisions. Work on your diction, tone, mode of delivery, pauses and clarity to make it more effective.

Maximise Communication. You are a communication antenna. You receive and radiate communication signals constantly. *We know communication is the essence of Interpersonal relationships.* If it is broken or distorted, the perception of the other party is similarly distorted, and you get the tasks, thoughts, aims, objectives, wishes, desires and needs of your boss or companion distorted. Work on the non-verbal part of it, as it constitutes more than 87 percent of communicational aspects. Your positive mannerism, body language, attitude and bearing will help you to get your viewpoint across in quicker timeframe.

Pursue Excellence. I know it is easier said than done. Nevertheless, if we constantly try to strive for it, *we in long term eliminate our negatives, which impede our work.* A draft well prepared does not require second or third correction; it saves time.

Break Big Projects. Break big projects into small achievable targets. One step at a time, keep on at it. It avoids frustrations and gives you the knowledge what has been logically achieved and what all is left to be achieved.

Turn the Heat On. If the engine of the car is not roaring or the rocket not fully aflame, they will not move or lift off. Turn the heat of your engines on. Only then will you move forward in life. Lazy cool man, paddling in the river of life, does not get fish to eat.

Time Your Aims. Like organising your daily routine, time your aims in life. On the bigger picture, you will know how close or far you are from your life objectives thus how hard or how much time you need to allocate for your self-actualisation.

Stick to a Plan. Once you have finalised a plan, to execute a particular task, stick to its essentials as per the thought out time line of action. Only make changes if the plan is not working. Midcourse corrections to bring forward or delay the schedule should not make you go into a frenzy of remaking the entire plan. A small correction to the original, in most of the cases, is more than enough.

Multitasking. It is an imbibed trait through cultures. Indians and Asians are very adept in this. My German brother-in-law and most of Europeans are confounded by the concept. Make yourself adept in multitasking. I find speaking on the phone, smoking, sipping tea and at the same time signing the routine letters quite doable. I think the Europeans, being perfectionists, go over board in seeking perfection; they have been so conditioned to think about and do one task at a time. When my brother-in-law drinks coffee he drinks coffee only. When he does work, he does work only to the tiniest detail. Not that I think it is wrong, but if it hampers you to do three other minor tasks on which an outcome of one big task is hinging, then I rather do multitasking than do one in so much detail that I forget or delay the start of the next important task by not executing three minor tasks.

And lastly

Increase Your Time Availability. We learnt earlier that the time given tó all the greatest achievers and the biggest failures was the same. How they utilised that time effectively was the key by which their destiny changed for better or worse. We have to increase the time available to us by beating the time trap and timing the time correctly. Let me explain it with the help of the diagrams below.

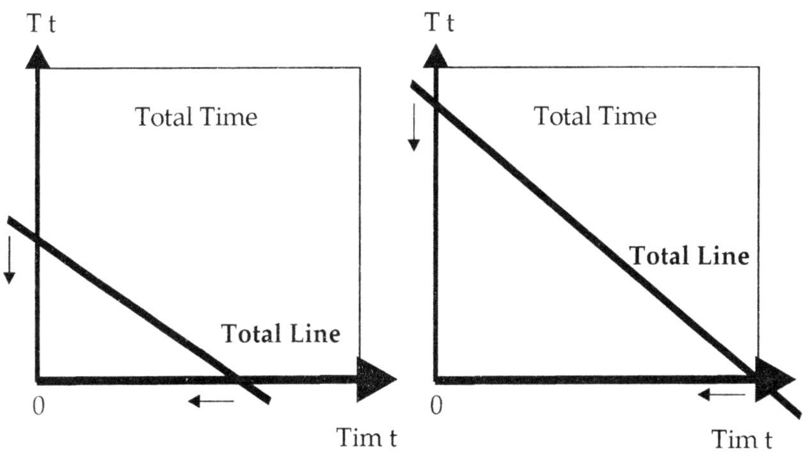

Total time in the life is the same. It is bounded by on y-axis by Tt which represents the trapped time and along the x-axis by Tim t, which represents the timing the perfect time i.e., taming it. If we get their values to minimum, our time availability automatically increases. Therefore, **our endeavour in life must always be out of the time trap and**

strive for taming the time by pushing the time line to zero.

My ninth elucidation to you is to imbibe and ingrain in your psyche the positive habits, which impart efficiency.

☆ ☆ ☆

"Suspect each moment,
For it is a thief,
Tiptoeing away,
With more than it brings."

— John Updike

CHAPTER 11

Embrace the Time Truths or be Timed Out

For the few, for whom this journey did not make any sense let me try to recapitulate what I have tried to tell, in a very abridged form. Hope the simplicity will not be missed out the second time.

- **Time is the destiny shaper of your life.**
- **We have only one life to live.**
- **We are time trapped.**

- **Time is not elastic. It cannot be stretched.**
- **Time is a constant.**
- **Time is a constant diminishing dimension.**
- **The day you were born, you were destined to die.**
- **You fool around with time; it will fool around with you.**
- **Great people knew the art of taming the time.**
- **Great people knew the value of time.**
- **Great people treated time as a science.**
- **Time management is a philosophy of life.**
- **Time management is life management.**
- **Time is the core of happiness.**
- **Time management is the cannon fodder of professionalism.**
- **Time is the key.**
- **Time is the support system of life.**
- **You are fixed in the spectrum of time.**
- **Timing the thoughts and the muscles to perform in synergy is the key.**
- **If we do not use the time effectively, we will be timed out in life.**
- **Mortality is our birthright.**
- **Fix your aims for your achievements, earlier the better.**

- The desires will act as stepping-stones to ultimately accomplish your aim
- It is time we started running the distance with times worth.
- Say hi, hi to high life.
- High life is a state of life you choose to live in. It is your internal ode to life; a prayer of having being blessed with this one life.
- High points in life leave an indelible impact on your balance life.
- We ordinary people have a very few high points in life to cherish. People who achieve a better hit-rate of high points in life, on the time line of life, than ordinary people like you and me are more satisfied.
- When we reduce the time distance between the high points in the life, we achieve a period of constant high life.
- We should strive for a period of high life.
- You have one life to achieve your dreams.
- You have to achieve your stated desires in life, and then increase your fruitful time you allocate to achieving your desires and also reduce your number of desires.
- We can also reduce the additional burden of time by fulfilling your desires the earliest.

- **Time reduces with astonishing speed when desires are left unfulfilled.**
- **The fact that when you need time the most, it is the least available commodity thus it is treacherous.**
- **Treacherous time and the treacherous times are interlinked and woven into the fabric of each other. The common thread, which binds them, strangely, is not the galloping technology, but the time itself.**
- **The time has been stolen out of your life.**
- **So many things to do and only one life to live.**
- **Where the hell or heavens is the time.**
- **The time is right in your hands.**
- **Time is in plenty but problem is only one. We just cannot find it. Where is the time?**
- **In less than a second, life flashes by.**
- **We are efficient and we do not waste time.**
- **We foresee ahead and plan ahead.**
- **We foresee our desires and plan ahead to fulfil those desires.**
- **Eliminate time, which offers no value.**
- **To tame time, tame yourself.**
- **To tame time, tame your unproductive desires.**

- To tame time, train yourself to tame yourself.
- To tame time, train yourself to expel the time wasters from your life.
- When you train, you actually tame yourself. It is that character you wish to mould.
- Training is essential to tame time and training is needed to tame time.
- You need to plan to save time thus tame time.
- Those people win, score high marks, and give fabulous presentations, for they practise or have it ingrained in their psyche, the art of managing time effectively.
- Can you fill the unforgiving minute, with sixty seconds worth of distance run.
- Time is very unforgiving.
- Time is a very precious commodity.
- Time gone cannot come back.
- We need to learn to time our time intelligently.
- Master the art of timing the right stroke at right time.
- When you time the time perfectly or to the optimum, you do not leave the ripples of wastage behind.
- In your daily routine, do you leave ripples of your incompetence behind?

- **Negative health is undue down time.**
- **Endeavour never to fall into the time trap.**
- **Endeavour always to tame time.**
- **Endeavour to increase your time availability.**
- **Let us be efficient to save time.**

I deliberately have taken the step to refocus your attention on what I have tried to say in the book.

It is for you to explore.

It is for you to dwell and ponder.

It is for you to find a meaning.

It is for you to find your answers.

I myself am a thirsty horse looking for a well to quench my thirst.

You have to reach that well yourself for I am too weak to lift your magnificent body.

My last and the final tenth commandment to you is, to start believing in yourself that you have the will to achieve your ultimate aims in life.

☆ ☆ ☆

"Time is of your own making,
Its clock ticks in your head.
The moment you stop thought,
Time too stops dead."

— Angelus Silesius

CHAPTER 12

Motivation

Whatever be the mumbo jumbo I tried to sell you, it has to come true, has to come from your inner core. It has to come from your inner urge to explore new horizons. My concept of motivation is not monetary, so help me God.

- **If you condition your mind and brain to one focus of thoughts, they get imprinted over your body cover, and come true.**
- **If you are dedicated to a cause, you can achieve your objective.**

- Unless you widen your horizons, you remain fixed to your minuscule self.
- All is possible, provided you have faith in your abilities.
- Your dreams or desires generally eat your finances.
- When you are focused and positive about life, you rub the goodness onto others.
- Are we living life or wasting life?
- Embrace high life.
- High periods in life make you immensely happy.
- High periods in life give you the confidence to face adversities bravely.
- High periods in life make difficult times look so ordinary.
- High periods in life make other life's moments worthy of being cherished.
- When we cherish simple things in life, which we have taken for granted, we could achieve a continuous cycle of high life.
- Men who do not work hard are generally classified, in the end of the day, as failures.
- When you are visionless and not focused then failure does beset you despite your hard work.

- **You have never lived unless you have almost died.**
- **You are trapped for lack of knowledge.**
- **You are trapped in excess of knowledge.**
- **You are time-trapped by the company you keep.**
- **You are afraid to explore new horizons.**
- **One life to live and so many things to experience.**
- **One life to live and so many things to do.**
- **I have only one life to live.**

Hope you have a new beginning as to how you have been perceiving about time and time available to achieve your objectives in life.

Hope you will see clearly the benefits of time management.

Hope you will be making time management as a philosophy of your life.

If you do not, you unquestionably will be timed out.

☆ ☆ ☆

Thou art energy, thou art time.
Thou art conquering power, thou art time.

— **The Author**

INDEX